A Hint

by Sidney Allen
illustrated by Kate Flanagan

Core Decodable 12

McGraw Hill Education

Bothell, WA • Chicago, IL • Columbus, OH • New York, NY

MHEonline.com

Send all inquiries to:
McGraw-Hill Education
8787 Orion Place
Columbus, OH 43240

ISBN: 978-0-02-144938-5
MHID: 0-02-144938-4

Printed in the United States of America.

7 8 9 LCR 25 24 23

Sid hid a hat.

"I had a hat," said Tim.

Dad had a hint.

"Hand him a hat, Sid," said Dad.

"A hat!" said Tim.

"Sid hid it!" said Dad.